SPOTLIGHT ON
THE ENGLISH CIVIL WAR

Tom Gibb

Wayland

SPOTLIGHT ON HISTORY

Spotlight on the Age of Exploration and Discovery
Spotlight on the Age of Revolution
Spotlight on the Agricultural Revolution
Spotlight on the Cold War
Spotlight on the Collapse of Empires
Spotlight on Elizabethan England
Spotlight on the English Civil War
Spotlight on the First World War
Spotlight on the Industrial Revolution
Spotlight on Industry in the Twentieth Century
Spotlight on Medieval Europe
Spotlight on Post-War Europe
Spotlight on the Reformation
Spotlight on Renaissance Europe
Spotlight on the Rise of Modern China
Spotlight on the Russian Revolution
Spotlight on the Second World War
Spotlight on the Victorians
Spotlight on the Age of Enlightenment
Spotlight on the Edwardians

First published in 1986 by Wayland (Publishers) Ltd
61 Western Road, Hove East Sussex BN3 1JD

Cover illustration: Cromwell at Dunbar by A. C. Gow

British Library Cataloguing in Publication Data
Gibb, Tom
Spotlight on the English civil war.—
(Spotlight on history)
1. Great Britain—History—Civil War,
I. Title II. Series 942.06′2 DA415

ISBN 0 85078 758 0

Printed in Great Britain at The Bath Press, Avon

CONTENTS

1 COURT AND COUNTRY

On the afternoon of 30 January 1649, Charles I was led through the corridors and halls of his palace at Whitehall to a large black scaffold in the courtyard. Seven years before he had walked through the same palace as master, but now his path was lined with the soldiers of his enemies. It was bitterly cold and the King had put on extra clothes, fearing that if he shivered the onlookers would think him afraid. A large crowd had gathered, but the scaffold was high above them and mounted soldiers stood between them and their King. Addressing those around him, Charles defended the actions of his reign, claiming he had only sought to uphold the liberties of his subjects. He reaffirmed his loyalty to the Church of England and begged the forgiveness of God for those who were about to execute him. Then,

King Charles I's execution in 1649. During the next eleven years no solution was found to the problem of how the country was to be run.

Queen Elizabeth I in procession: many people looked back to her time to solve the problems of the relationship between monarch and Parliament.

taking off his cloak, he knelt at the block. It took the executioner only one strike of the axe to behead him. A boy of seventeen, an eyewitness, later recalled the crowd's reaction as the axe fell: 'Such a groan as I never heard before, and desire I may never hear again.'

Less than eleven years earlier Charles had told one of his nephews, that he was the 'happiest King in Christendom'. Since that time, however, he had faced rebellion, battle, imprisonment, escape and trial before finally coming to the scaffold. His defeat and subsequent execution by Parliament is one of the most extraordinary stories of British history, and played a key part in the country's development.

The monarchy

Britain today is a monarchy, but the monarch's powers are limited. Technically it is the Queen who appoints new prime ministers and gives her assent to all new laws, but in practice it is Parliament, and more specifically the House of Commons, which is sovereign. By custom the Queen is obliged to appoint a prime minister who has the support of the majority of those in the Commons. And, in practice, the Queen never vetoes Parliamentary bills.

In the seventeenth century the relationship between monarch and Parliament was much more vague. Britain has never had a written constitution so there was no clear document to refer to when disputes arose as to who should levy taxes, who should be responsible for the defence of the realm and raising armies, who should make and enforce the laws, who should decide the religion of the country and all the other things for which governments are responsible. Everything was settled by custom and reference to the past, which of course gave much scope for disagreement.

It was to the reign of Elizabeth I that many turned when seeking the answers to these questions. The powers she exercised as queen, independently of Parliament, were called her Prerogative. She was responsible for the defence of the realm and could declare war or make peace. It was her navy which defeated the Spanish Armada in 1588 and she was supreme commander of the armed forces. She decided the religion of the country, appointing the bishops who made church policy. She was thought to be the source of all justice and could hear cases directly in what were called the Prerogative Courts. She also appointed the judges to the other courts and could issue proclamations (or orders to her subjects) which in effect had the force of laws.

While Elizabeth jealously guarded her powers she was also careful not to overstep the mark and encroach on her subjects' liberties. It was never thought that the monarch had unlimited powers and there were time-honoured ways in which the 'Governance of the Realm' should be carried out. In practice Elizabeth had to rely on her subjects to maintain her authority, for it was they who carried out the orders. There was no professional or paid administration, such as the Civil Service today, and there was no standing army.

The House of Commons, the lower chamber of Parliament, at the time of King Charles I.

The peasants and ordinary townspeople of Britain played little direct part in politics.

Court and country

At the centre of royal government was the Privy Council. Made up of the principal ministers and favourites of the king, it was here that most policy was debated and most influence could be exerted on the king. There was intense competition at the court to get a place on the council, both from those who wanted to influence policy and those who wanted to make their fortunes. Anyone with influence could expect large financial rewards, part of which they would in turn pass on to others, building up their own network of supporters both at court and in the country. The whole system worked on 'perks', gifts and bribes.

In the country it was the nobility and gentry who maintained order and carried out the commands of central government. From these, the king chose the principal officers of each county, the Lord Lieutenant, the Sheriffs and Justices of the Peace (JPs), although in practice most of the leading gentry of the shire would be on the bench of JPs. These men collected the taxes, dealt with criminal cases, mustered the local levies for the king's armies and dealt with all the other chores of government. They were unpaid amateurs who did the job because their status in society dictated that they should. No king could hope to rule without their support, and as Charles was to discover, their goodwill was something he could ill afford to lose.

These then were the rulers—or 'Political Nation'—and below them the common people played little direct part in politics. As a contemporary noted: 'they care not what government they live under so long as they may plough and go to market.' Many were illiterate and to them the court must have seemed far away. But they were deeply conscious of the place in society to which they had been born, and it was this recognition of order and hierarchy which kept society together.

The Church

By the time Charles I came to the throne in 1625, Europe had been divided between Protestants and Catholics for over a century. A bloody war (the Thirty Years War 1618–48) was now raging across Europe which many regarded as the final great struggle between the two religions. It is against this background of fear and hatred that events in England took shape.

Although Henry VIII had broken from Rome in the 1530s, the Church of England still bore much resemblance in organization to the Catholic Church. The hierarchy of bishops and clergy, the church ceremonies, altars and images were to many Protestants superstitious remnants of the hated Church of Rome. The more radical Protestants, nicknamed 'Puritans', believed that these barriers between the true believer and God would lead only to the eternal fires of hell.

Many wanted to rebuild the Church completely, along the lines suggested by the great reformer John Calvin, with preaching ministers and lay elders enforcing a uniform Protestant doctrine. They did not like the current prayer book because it was open to too many interpretations. Others, however, wanted more religious freedom to choose their own ministers and follow their own consciences. This fragile religious peace was to be broken under Charles I.

Radical protestants, nicknamed Puritans, disagreed with other religious factions.

These two city merchants held the monopoly on the wine trade in the 1640s, thus forcing other tradesmen out of business.

Parliament

Parliament was the great forum where the political nation met. It had three parts—the king, the House of Lords (made up of the nobility and the bishops), and the House of Commons. Its main function was to make laws, which, until they were passed were known as bills. Bills started in the Commons, and then had to be passed by both the Lords and the king before they became full Acts of Parliament and part of the law. In this way the monarch could always veto bills. It was also the monarch's decision when Parliament was to be called and when dissolved.

The other main function of Parliament was to provide the king with extra taxation in times of emergency. It was the Commons who voted these taxes, called subsidies, and as the crown's finances grew weaker, so the influence of the Commons grew stronger.

The crown's main income came from customs duties on imports and exports, and from land. As the crown's need for income increased, Queen Elizabeth I and King James I had resorted to other, very unpopular, measures to raise money. They sold monopolies—the exclusive right to manufacture and sell certain goods—to royal favourites. These monopolies destroyed other people's trade and livelihoods. Also to raise money, they had reintroduced old feudal taxes, sold land, titles and knighthoods, and raised forced loans from merchants.

The Commons became increasingly reluctant to grant further money but the crown, heavily in debt, could not hope to reform its ways without some new source of income. Nor, as Charles was to discover, could it hope to fight a war.

2 CHARLES I

King Charles I was a deeply religious man who took the high responsibilities of his office very seriously. He believed passionately that he had been given his authority by God, and that those who questioned it also questioned the Divine will. But just as his subjects were accountable to him, so also, he believed, was he accountable to God and would be called to judgement for the way he ruled. Charles believed it was his duty to preserve intact the rights of the crown and the Church of England, so they could be handed on to his successors. His belief in this theory of the Divine Right of Kings was totally inflexible and he was prepared to die rather than give it up.

The early Parliaments

When Charles opened his reign in 1625 with a war against Spain, England's traditional enemy, it should have been a popular policy with his Protestant subjects. Unfortunately, however, the war was a disaster and England found herself fighting France as well as Spain. Various expeditions were led with great incompetence by Charles's favourite, the Duke of Buckingham, and many of the soldiers who returned defeated died of hunger and disease because there was not enough money to pay them. No-one wanted to pay for such an unsuccessful war. In desperation Charles forced civilians to give free food and accommodation to his soldiers, imprisoning any who refused.

Against this background, relations with the Parliaments he called to vote taxes for the war grew worse and worse. The Commons tried to impeach Buckingham, a process whereby they could bring a member of the upper house to trial before the rest of the Lords with themselves prosecuting. They refused to grant the King any money and produced a Petition of Right against the abuses of the King's government. Charles accepted the petition but he still received no money. Finally in 1629 he decided to make peace and rule without the help of Parliament.

'The Eleven Years Tyranny'

The eleven years of personal rule after 1629 was later called the 'Eleven Years Tyranny', but there is little evidence it was viewed in this way at the time. The principal grievance of the 1620s (the monopoly of power held by Buckingham) was removed when he was assassinated in 1628. Some of those who had led the Parliamentary opposition now joined the King's government, the most notable being Thomas

Charles I, whose belief in the Divine Right of Kings was so profound that he was prepared to die rather than give it up.

George Villiers, First Duke of Buckingham and favourite of Charles, was at the centre of the King's troubles with Parliament in the 1620s.

Wentworth, later Earl of Strafford.

Attempts were made to tighten up the administration. A detailed instruction manual, called *The Book of Orders*, was written for JPs. Far more use was made of the courts which relied directly on the King's authority (Prerogative Courts). The main one was called the Star Chamber, which was in fact just the King sitting with his councillors as a court. But there was also the Church Court of High Commission and the Councils of the North and Ireland. Wentworth in particular earned a reputation for strong government as Lord President of the North and later Lord Deputy in Ireland. However, there was a limit to what the King could do without a professional administration. He still relied on the ordinary gentry to do most of the work and did not have enough money to change this.

Ship Money

Charles I's decision to rule without Parliament meant he had to find money elsewhere. All the old financial abuses which Parliaments had complained about were continued, and even extended. Most alarming for the believers in constitutional government, the King used his prerogative to start collecting a tax called Ship Money throughout the country, without the consent of Parliament. Previously it had been collected only in the ports. If the King could impose a new tax at will, where would this leave the property rights of the subject?

In fact Ship Money, which was used to build up the navy, was a very reasonable tax. Towns on the south coast were being attacked by pirates from North Africa and their inhabitants taken off as slaves. English merchants needed protection from the aggressive Dutch. The enlarged navy soon brought results and the slaves were returned after a treaty was forced on the pirates. Indeed Ship Money seems to have been one of the best collected taxes the crown had ever had, with nearly ninety per cent being paid until 1637. When a rich Buckinghamshire landowner, John Hampden, tried to get it declared illegal the judges supported the King. It was only when the money started to be used for other purposes that men refused to pay.

Thomas Wentworth, Earl of Strafford, Charles' chief minister, was put on trial by Parliament and beheaded when the King failed to save him.

The House of Lords, the upper chamber of Parliament, with King Charles surrounded by peers.

Laud and the Puritans

Charles I had been brought up in the Church of England and was very attached to its ceremonies and forms of worship. Over the previous century the Church had been pillaged of much of its wealth and land by the crown and the landed gentry. Many of the clergy were very poor and badly educated. Charles wished to restore the prestige of the Church and also clarify its doctrines, which were very vague. He disliked the ideas of the Calvinists who believed in the doctrine of predestination (that all people are predestined from the beginning of time to go to heaven or hell and have no free will to act and decide their own fate). Instead he promoted followers of the Dutch theologian Arminius who believed in free will, and these now started to claim that the Calvinists were outside the scope of the Anglican Church.

In William Laud, Charles found an Arminian Archbishop of Canterbury after his own heart. Together they used the royal authority to try to restore the Church and silence the Calvinists and other radical Protestants. Altars, organs, and images were returned to churches, private preaching was banned, and laws which made everyone attend church were enforced. Those who disobeyed were called before the Prerogative Courts and punished.

But the deep-seated beliefs of many of the King's subjects could not be uprooted so easily. Many Calvinists were wealthy and influential men who were outraged to be suddenly branded as 'Puritans'. Worst of all, while the King persecuted Protestants, he appeared to let Catholics do as they pleased. He had married a French Catholic Princess, Henrietta Maria, who kept a large Catholic following at court. Fines imposed on Catholics under Elizabeth I were not collected. Charles even began to use his navy to help the hated Spanish supply their armies in the Netherlands in return for money.

The Navy, which Charles so carefully built up with Ship Money, sided with Parliament.

William Laud, Archbishop of Canterbury, was an enemy of Calvinism; like others of Charles' ministers he met his death by execution on Tower Hill.

Henrietta Maria, Charles' French-born wife, was unpopular with many because she kept a large Roman Catholic following at court.

Often the radical Protestants could count on popular support. In the most famous case three Puritan preachers, Bastwicke, Burton and Prynne, were sentenced by Star Chamber to have their ears cut off and be put up for public mockery. But this only gave them the chance to preach to a large sympathetic crowd who saw them as martyrs against the King's cruel archbishop.

In fact Charles never leaned towards Catholicism, although he did seem to regard its errors as only minor compared with those of the Puritans. But if his policies aroused the suspicions and prejudices of his English subjects, his problems were nothing compared to those he faced when he turned his attention to Scotland.

3 THE END OF THE KING'S PEACE

The kingdoms of England and Scotland were not united until 1603, when James I came to the throne. Although they then shared the same king they retained different laws, a separate parliament and, much to Charles's dislike, a different Church. The Kirk, as it was called in Scotland, had undergone a full Calvinist reformation in the sixteenth century. Godly ministers kept a watchful eye over the morals of their flocks and the Sabbath day of rest was strictly enforced. James I managed to reintroduce bishops, who were useful royal servants in government, but had stopped short of bringing in the other services and ceremonies of the Anglican Church, knowing the opposition they would generate. Charles was not so cautious.

The first Bishops' War

When the King ordered the Anglican prayer book to be read throughout Scotland in July 1637, many ministers refused to use it. Where they did try, their attempts were greeted with riots. The ministers and the powerfully independent nobility set about organizing resistance. A document of 1580, claimed to be the founding charter of the Kirk,

John Pym played a crucial role in the survival of Parliament's cause until his death at the end of 1643.

Ier.50.5. Come let us joyn our selves to the Lord

16 a Solemn 43

LEAGVE AND COVENANT,

for Reformation, and defence of Religion, the Honour and happinesse of the king, and the Peace and safety of the three kingdoms of

ENGLAND, SCOTLAND, and IRELAND.

in a perpetuall Covenant that shall not be forgotten.

We Noblemen, Barons, Knights, Gentlemen, Citizens, Burgesses, Ministers of the Gospel, and Commons of all sorts in the Kingdoms of England, Scotland, *and* Ireland, *by the Providence of God living under one King, and being of one reformed Religion, having before our eyes the Glory of God, and the advancement of the Kingdome of our Lord and Saviour Jesus Christ, the Honour and happinesse of the kings Majesty and his posterity, and the true publique Liberty, Safety, and Peace of the Kingdoms, wherein every ones private Condition is included, and calling to minde the treacherous and bloody Plots, Conspiracies, Attempts, and Practices of the Enemies of God, against the true Religion, and professors thereof in all places, especially in these three kingdoms ever since the Reformation of Religion, and how much their rage, power and presumption, are of late, and at this time increased and exercised; whereof the deplorable state of the Church and kingdom of* Ireland, *the distressed estate of the Church and kingdom of* England, *and the dangerous estate of the Church and kingdom of* Scotland, *are present and publique Testimonies; We have now at last, (after other means of Supplication, Remonstrance, Protestations, and Sufferings) for the preservation of our selves and our Religion, from utter Ruine and Destruction; according to the commendable practice of these Kingdoms in former times, and the Example of Gods people in other Nations; After mature deliberation, resolved and determined to enter into a mutuall and solemn League and Covenant; Wherein we all subscribe, and each one of us for himself, with our hands lifted up to the most high God, do sweare;*

The Covenant was claimed to be the founding charter of the Scottish Church (the Kirk).

was revived. The Covenant, as it became known, reaffirmed the full Calvinist structure and theology of the Kirk, and all over Scotland crowds flocked to sign it.

The strength of opposition took Charles by surprise, but he nevertheless determined to quash the rebellion. 'Not anything can reduce this people but only force' he wrote. The trouble was, he was unprepared and the Covenanters had plenty of time to fully reorganize the Kirk and recruit and train an army. When Charles's army did march north in 1639, it met with disaster. The cavalry under the frivolous Lord Holland crossed the border into Scotland way ahead of the infantry. When they came across the Scots army, well drawn up around banners proudly stamped with the words 'For Christ's Crown and Covenant', the English horse fled back across the River Tweed. The English were clearly outnumbered by the better armed and organized Covenanters and in the end Charles had to negotiate. At the Pacification of Berwick he promised the Scots he would call an assembly of the Kirk and a Parliament to discuss the issue.

The Short Parliament

In fact, the King was only playing for time. Thomas Wentworth was recalled from Ireland and, while the Scots Parliament met to discuss terms for peace, he urged Charles to call a Parliament in England to vote money for war. Wentworth believed he could control the English Parliament, but he underestimated the strength of opposition to royal policies. The King was favouring Catholics at home, using his navy to ferry Spanish soldiers and bullion to the Netherlands and now making war on his Protestant Scottish subjects.

The unrest showed itself first of all in a growing tax strike against Ship Money. When Charles tried to add a similar tax to pay for his army, called 'Coat and Conduct Money', people simply refused to pay. More seriously, the JPs and Sheriffs refused to co-operate in collecting it. By 1640, when Parliament met, no-one was paying either tax and for the first time there seems to have been a concerted campaign by opponents of royal policy in the elections to the House of Commons. Foremost amongst these were the members of the Providence Island Company, a group of strongly Protestant nobility and gentry who had set up 'Godly' colonies in the New World to attack the Spanish. The Commons fell under the leadership of the secretary of the company, John Pym, who immediately set about organizing petitions against abuses. Not surprisingly, Parliament refused to give taxes to pay for the war. It was even rumoured that its leaders were in secret communication with the Scots and preparing to raise the Covenanters' grievances as well as their own.

After less than a month Charles dissolved Parliament. On the advice of Wentworth, who had recently been made Earl of Strafford, he arrested its leaders and prepared to attack the Scots. Strafford made plans to bring over an Irish army, mainly made up of Catholics.

Despite Strafford's efforts, which included imprisoning London aldermen to force them to pay a loan and summarily executing youths after riots in the city, the war was another disaster. The Scots invaded England, routed the English vanguard at Newburn and took the city of Newcastle. Once again Charles had to talk. By the Treaty of Ripon he agreed to call a Parliament in England and pay the occupying Scots army a subsidy of £25,000 a month.

The trial of Strafford

The leaders of the Parliament which met in November 1640 were precisely the men Charles had locked up earlier that year. Nearly all the MPs supported the attack on the King's policy. In the first week the Commons received over twenty petitions from the counties against Ship Money, innovations in religion, Star Chamber and the like. But most of the political nation only wanted a return to what they saw as the traditional balance between crown and Parliament, not any radical change. The story of the next eighteen months is of the rise of a Royalist party. They came to support the crown as it became increasingly clear that Pym and the other activists were prepared to sponsor a huge alteration in that balance, rather than allow Charles to regain his power.

At first Pym was able to unite both houses by an attack on the King's ministers. The King's secretary, Windebank, and the Lord Chief Justice Finch—who had declared the legality of Ship Money—fled to the Continent. Strafford, who had earned the nickname 'Black Tom Tyrant', and his friend Laud were impeached and sent to the Tower. Laud was to remain there until his execution in 1645, but the Commons were not content to leave Strafford so long.

Strafford's trial started in March 1642 with the Commons prosecuting. They alleged that he had intended using the Irish Catholic army to subdue the King's peaceful subjects in England, clearly a treasonable crime. But they had only the unsupported evidence of one witness, whereas Strafford was able to call several councillors to testify in his defence. With no real evidence the impeachment failed. Undeterred, Pym introduced another device called a Bill of Attainder. This no longer needed to prove Strafford legally guilty, but only to show that his death was necessary for the safety of the State. However, like any other bill it needed to be passed by both the Lords and the King before it became an Act.

Evidence of the Queen's unpopularity: this woodcut shows 'Great Charles, our Gracious King, eclipsed by the seductive persuasion of his Queen'.

The execution of the Earl of Strafford on Tower Hill in 1641 was an event for which Charles I could never forgive himself.

Once again Strafford defended himself with great ability when the bill reached the Lords. Many were now alarmed at such an open attack on one of their number and at the lengths to which Pym was going to destroy the King's power. Parliament had already taken over the collection of taxes, giving the King only a small allowance. They were issuing orders to the King's officers in the counties and effectively claiming a veto over ministers they did not like.

But Pym kept up the pressure on the upper house. There had by this time been a complete change of power in the city of London, which had its own independent government. Committed Protestants who supported Pym now held a majority on the most powerful body in the city, the Common Council. Large numbers of the labourers, or apprentices as they were called, who worked in the port and industries of the capital were mobilized by rumours of popish plots to kill Parliament's leaders. Mobs of apprentices swarmed around Parliament, shouting for Strafford's blood and threatening the peers with violence. The King then made a bad mistake: he promised the Lords that he would never let Strafford be executed. In the vote which followed many loyal peers abstained, fearful of the mobs, and safe in the knowledge that the King would veto the bill. The trouble was, Charles did not veto it. Strafford very bravely wrote to the King, telling him to sign the death warrant to stop the riots. Under pressure from all sides, Charles gave in and Strafford was beheaded on May 12. It was a decision for which Charles never forgave himself. Later when he himself stood on the scaffold, he blamed his fate on his disloyalty to his servant: 'An unjust sentence that I suffered for to take effect is punished now by an unjust sentence on me.'

4 THE ROAD TO WAR

A few months after Strafford's death a contemporary wrote that Pym and his friends had made themselves 'so obnoxious and guilty to the King' that they could never feel safe from his vengeance if he regained his power. Charles continued to give concessions but they were meaningless in terms of reaching a settlement. He agreed to the abolition of the Prerogative Courts and to bills which forced him to call a Parliament every three years and stopped him from dissolving Parliament without its consent. This allowed the present Parliament to stay in existence until 1653, thus earning the name 'the Long Parliament.' But Charles, convinced of his duty to preserve the crown's authority, would almost certainly have reversed these concessions if given the chance. Few of his enemies trusted him.

Archibald Campbell, the 8th Earl of Argyll, was the head of the Campbell clan and a leading Covenanter.

James Graham, Marquis of Montrose, led Royalist support in Scotland and proved himself a master of guerrilla warfare.

Scotland and Ireland

In the summer of 1641 Charles travelled to Scotland to try and gain the support of the Covenanters against his enemies in England. Despite being showered with rewards the leading Covenanter and head of the Campbell Clan, the Earl of Argyll, clearly did not trust Charles. Meanwhile those who might have formed a royalist party in Scotland were given no support. In particular the Marquis of Montrose, a popular figure, was left to languish in jail where he had been locked up by Argyll after showing royalist sympathies.

Whilst the King feted his past enemies in Scotland, Ireland exploded into rebellion. For the last half century Protestant settlers had been driving the native Catholics from their land. Strafford had to some extent held them in check, but with his death the situation got out of control. Fearing the consequences for themselves if the Puritans came to power in England, the Irish Catholics rebelled, claiming they had the support of the King. Although the royal warrants the rebels showed were clearly forgeries, the Irish rebellion provided Pym with fresh ammunition as Parliament met that autumn. Most Englishmen regarded the Irish with a mixture of fear and hatred.

The Grand Remonstrance

The Irish rebellion brought into focus the King's last remaining powers —to appoint his own ministers and command the army. By this time both houses were seriously divided. A group around Lord Falkland and Edward Hyde had accepted office in the King's government and did not want to see more radical change. Playing the good Protestant the King asked Parliament for money to raise an army for restoring order in Ireland. Pym feared, quite justifiably, that it might be used to destroy opposition in England and Scotland first. To unite his supporters a Grand Remonstrance was prepared in the Commons, condemning in detail royal policy over the whole length of the reign. Its purpose was to show beyond question that Charles was unfit to appoint his own councillors or command the army. But the growing strength of the Royalists was demonstrated when the Commons passed the Grand Remonstrance by only eleven votes at one o'clock in the morning.

The Archbishop of Canterbury's house, Lambeth Palace, under attack by a crowd of Londoners in 1642.

A satirical cartoon drawn by a contemporary artist showing the antipathy between Cavaliers and Roundheads.

In the Lords, Pym had already lost control. Whilst the bishops still retained their seats, the Lords would block any initiatives passed by the Commons. Once again mobs of apprentices swarmed around Parliament shouting 'No Bishops!' But all the time the King was preparing to counter-attack. He had regained control of the Tower and sent out orders for absent MPs to return to Westminster. Most would be on his side and he hoped he would soon have a majority in the Commons. He also replaced the local London Soldiers (The London Trained Bands) who had been guarding Westminster and were sympathetic to Pym, with a regiment loyal to the crown.

Roundheads and Cavaliers

Over Christmas the rioting grew worse. It was then that the nicknames of Cavalier and Roundhead were born in scuffles between the King's officers and the apprentices. Both were terms of abuse, Roundhead referring to the shorn hairstyle of the apprentices, and Cavalier being a mispronunciation of *Caballero*, the hated Spanish trooper and oppressor of Protestants.

It was also at this troubled time that the British press was born. A weekly pamphlet reporting on Parliament was soon followed by a whole host of similar pamphlets in fierce competiton with each other. But unfortunately the King was slow to catch on, not realizing the power of this new weapon. Most of the pamphlets supported Pym and gave him a crucial edge in the propaganda battle to win the support of London.

London lost

With time running out Pym forced the King to make his move. He knew he could count on the support of London, where the Royalists were outnumbered and demoralized. If he could show that the King was prepared to use force and totally disregard the privileges of Parliament, then he would demonstrate the hollowness of all the concessions Charles had made. Pym hoped the city would then rise in support

Roundhead troops: a mounted officer with foot soldiers including a pikeman and a musketeer.

A Cavalier: the feathers, ribbons and lace contrast strongly with the plain simplicity of Puritan clothing.

The King arrives at the House of Commons to arrest Pym and four other members, only to find that they have already escaped.

of Parliament. At the end of December the bishops were impeached and sent to the Tower. Then, at the beginning of January, Pym threatened to impeach Charles's Queen, Henrietta Maria.

With the Queen under threat Charles could wait no longer. His supporters in the Lords accused Pym and four other members of the Commons of High Treason, but unfortunately for the Royalist cause, failed to get them sent to the Tower. Instead of going into hiding Pym stayed in the House, guessing the King would use force to try and get him and his fellows out. The King fell for the bait. He went personally with a company of soldiers to make the arrest. If he succeeded he knew the opposition would fall apart, but it was a big risk.

The attempt failed. As Charles entered the front of the House Pym and his men were escaping down the river on a barge. The King could only admit defeat with the words: 'All my birds have flown'.

The King had lost London. Barricades were set up and manned by the London Trained Bands who were now in open rebellion. Crowds filled the streets shouting 'Privilege!' Parliament withdrew to the Guildhall in the City for protection against the King. Those of his supporters who remained, and they included the Mayor of the city, were outnumbered and demoralized. On January 10 Charles left his capital. England was slipping into civil war.

5 THE FIRST CAMPAIGNS

The night King Charles raised his standard at Nottingham, on 22 August 1642, there was a dreadful storm which blew the standard down again. Many of his supporters saw this as a bad omen. Charles' position in the country was not strong for, although he still had many supporters in the south, they had no rallying point. His enemies held all the main ports, including London and Bristol and the navy, which Charles had so carefully built up with Ship Money, also rebelled. Without the navy's support, large-scale help from abroad would be difficult.

Having fled from London, Charles I set up his standard in Nottingham, in August 1642.

Sir Edmund Verney was one of many who, out of loyalty to the King, took part in a civil war he hated.

Taking sides

The news of the split between the King and his Parliament was greeted in the provinces with disbelief and dismay. Both sides sent out commissioners to recruit, but the call to arms was not enthusiastically taken up. Local loyalties were still strongest and the majority of the gentry now retreated behind county boundaries, not anxious to start fighting their neighbours and fellow Englishmen. In no less than twenty-four counties the gentry made pacts amongst themselves to remain neutral. Some even got as far as raising a third force to repel invaders.

But although the majority did not want a war, fighting nevertheless broke out. It seems those with strong religious convictions were the first to take up arms—Catholics and high church Anglicans joining the King, and convinced Protestants joining Parliament. Gradually they forced everyone else to choose sides, treating those who claimed neutrality as enemies. No clear pattern can be seen in the division, and the 'political nation' was split down the middle. Many joined whichever side was most powerful in their area and did as little as possible. Others followed family traditions of service to the crown or Parliament. Most hoped the war would be over in a few months.

Sir Edward Verney must have echoed the thoughts of many as he joined the King at Nottingham: 'For my part I do not like the quarrel,' he said, 'and do heartily wish the King would yield and consent to what they demand.' He took up arms from personal loyalty to the King, saying: 'I have eaten his bread and served him near thirty years and will not do so base a thing as to foresake him; and rather chose to lose my life, which I am sure I shall do . . .' Sir Edward did indeed

The Battle of Edgehill where Sir Edmund Verney fell, bravely defending the King's standard while the Royalist flank was temporarily unprotected.

lose his life a few months later, bravely defending the standard at the battle of Edgehill. Like many on both sides he died for a cause in which it seems he only half believed.

Warfare

The majority of Englishmen had no direct experience of war, but they had only to look to the Continent to see the likely effects. Over the past decades Germany had been ravaged by the largely mercenary armies battling for control of Europe. They were given a free hand to kill, rape and pillage, and horrific stories came out of Germany of whole cities destroyed by the rampaging armies.

In England war was conducted less brutally. It was very mobile with armies often marching great distances. Although a strong castle could hold out for some time, no walls could withstand artillery indefinitely. Neither was there any clearly dominant weapon on the battlefield. Firearms were very inaccurate and slow to load. Well-drilled infantry could often do much better with a long spear called a pike. Perhaps the most dramatic weapon was the cavalry charge. Few could withstand the impact of closely packed troopers charging at the gallop. But they had to be well used, needing space to manoeuvre, and they could not attack pikemen head on. They were also hard to control and keep together in the din of battle. Much depended on the training and discipline of the soldiers and the skill of the generals in picking the best ground to fight on. Once battle was started events became very confusing and often the day was decided by the quick thinking and courage of individual commanders.

A pikeman, or foot soldier, of Cromwell's army and a musketeer aiming his cumbersome weapon.

Edgehill

One of those supporters to join Charles at Nottingham was his nephew Prince Rupert of the Rhine. This bold and daring young soldier set about turning the King's cavalry into a force to be reckoned with—putting 'spirit into the King's army, that all men seemed resolved'. By contrast the confidence of the Parliamentary commander, the Earl of Essex, was very low. When he left London in September with a large but untrained army, he took with him his coffin and winding sheet. He had orders to rescue the King and his sons 'out of the hands of those desperate persons who were then about them,' and bring them home to their 'loving Parliament'.

As Essex approached, the King had to retreat to the Welsh borders to seek more recruits. At the first skirmish at Powick Bridge, Rupert's cavalry smashed a much larger force in a single charge. By mid October, 1642, the tables were turned and the King started to march on London with over 13,000 men. Essex hastened to cut him off but missed, and on the morning of the 23 October he woke to find the royal army had occupied a slope called Edgehill which dominated the road to Banbury, Oxford and London.

Both sides formed up traditionally with the main body of infantry in the centre protected by cavalry on either flank. In a way that was to become all too familiar, the Royalist commanders started off by arguing and the commander-in-chief, the Earl of Lindsey, resigned

A cavalry charge at the Battle of Edgehill, after which both King and Parliament claimed victory.

Prince Rupert of the Rhine, Charles' nephew, was a bold, daring and sometimes headstrong commander nicknamed 'The Mad Cavalier'.

when the King accepted Rupert's advice. Many of the Royalists disliked this proud young foreigner.

The battle opened with an unstoppable charge by Rupert's Cavaliers which routed most of the Parliamentary horse. Parts of the infantry also started to flee and for a moment it looked as if the battle and the war were over. But for the presence of mind of Sir William Balfour, who kept a large body of Parliament's cavalry in reserve, it probably would have been. As Rupert's followers went charging off the field, caught up in the heat of the chase, Balfour attacked the unprotected flank of the King's infantry. The standard fell with its bearer, Sir Edward Verney, killed. For a moment the King was in danger of capture. Only the return of Rupert's horsemen prevented defeat and as night fell both armies drew off exhausted.

Both sides claimed a victory, but with the road to London open the Royalists had the tactical advantage. However, Charles failed to take this opportunity, despite his nephew's urging. Instead, he moved slowly. By the time he reached what is now Heathrow, Essex had overtaken him and was already in London. Alarmed by stories of Royalist looting, the merchants of the capital rallied to the cause. The trained bands and Essex's army formed up outside the City so that the King, badly outnumbered, had to retreat to his new capital at Oxford. At the end of 1642, London, the home counties, East Anglia and much of the Midlands were under Parliament's control and were to remain so for the rest of the war.

6 THE WAR SPREADS

The summer of 1643 was a bad time for Parliament. Their main army under Essex had tried to advance towards Oxford but had been halted by a series of lightning raids down the Thames Valley by Prince Rupert. Complaining bitterly about the lack of money to pay his troops, Essex retreated and refused to co-operate with the other commanders. The news which came in from them was even more alarming.

'This war without an enemy'
In the south-west the popular Royalist leader Sir Ralph Hopton had raised an army of tough Cornishmen. After routing a force twice the size of his own he marched into Devon and met up with two other Royalist armies, one of them commanded by Rupert's younger brother Prince Maurice. This powerful force now threatened the second port of the kingdom at Bristol.

Sir Ralph Hopton, a popular general and leader of Royalist support in the south-west of England.

Sir William Waller, a leader of the Parliamentary troops, had fought alongside his Royalist enemy Sir Ralph Hopton in the German wars.

Alarmed at the danger, Parliament's commander in the Midlands, Sir William Waller, hurried south. By one of the ironies of the war, Waller and Hopton were in fact old friends, having fought together in the German wars, but they now faced each other as enemies. Hoping perhaps to change his friend's loyalty, Hopton wrote to Waller and suggested they meet to talk. Waller turned the offer down saying he must remain true to the cause he now served. But his reply showed the anguish felt by many on both sides:

'That Great God, which is the searcher of my heart, knows with what a sad sense I go upon this service, and with what a perfect hatred I detest this war without an enemy . . . We are both upon the stage and must act those parts that are assigned us in this tragedy; let us do it in a way of honour, and without personal animosities, whatsoever the issue be . . .'

The Battle of Lansdown Hill, one of the hardest-fought encounters of the War.

The ensuing battle on Lansdown Hill above Bath was one of the hardest-fought in the war. By nightfall Hopton's Cornish pikemen had won the ridge, but with a terrible loss of life.

Waller fell back for reinforcements from Bristol and when he again advanced the Royalists were in no condition to fight. Sending the cavalry to Oxford for help, Hopton took refuge behind the walls of Devizes. Two days later the relief force arrived and though still badly outnumbered attacked Waller's surprised army. After a series of Royalist cavalry charges, the battle on Roundway Down turned into a rout and Parliament lost its entire western army.

Prince Rupert was quick to join the victorious army and immediately marched on Bristol. On the 26 July they stormed the city, the Cornishmen once again ignoring serious losses. After Rupert's cavalry broke through, the city surrendered and the parliamentary garrison marched out, leaving their weapons behind. The King now held a port to challenge the strength of London.

The news was equally bad for the Parliamentarians from other areas of the country. In the north the Royalist Marquis of Newcastle had defeated Sir Thomas Fairfax and his father, and was now besieging them in Hull. Even puritan East Anglia, where the Earl of Manchester and his able second-in-command Oliver Cromwell were cementing a powerful alliance of counties for Parliament (called the Eastern

Association) suddenly looked weak. The port of King's Lynn declared for the King, and there was a serious Royalist rising in Norfolk. If Newcastle came to their aid the very heartland of Parliament's territory would be threatened.

The saving of Gloucester

Whilst Pym battled at Westminster to keep control amid the arguments and recriminations which followed defeat, the King turned his attention to the Puritan city of Gloucester, which controlled the trade route down the River Severn to his new port of Bristol. However, the young Colonel Massey, who commanded the city, defied the King's demands of surrender and, aided by the Godly citizens, set about organizing its defence. Meanwhile there was frantic activity in London to raise an army for the relief of Gloucester. The quarrels were put to one side and for the time Pym reasserted control.

Essex left London towards the end of August and after a forced march of twelve days appeared over the hills above the Severn Valley. He arrived none too soon, for the defenders had only three barrels of powder left when the King's army was forced to withdraw. With Gloucester safe, Essex now hurried back towards London, on the way getting the better of the King's army, who tried to cut him off at Newbury, south of Oxford. He entered the capital as a conquering hero.

King Charles and a group of supporters being refused entry to the city of Hull by Parliamentary forces in 1642.

Cromwell at the Battle of Marston Moor, where his Ironsides defeated the Royalist forces.

As winter approached there was good news for the Parliamentarians from East Anglia as well. Newcastle failed to exploit the Royalist rising, wasting his energy on a costly siege of Hull. The rising was put down by the Earl of Manchester and Oliver Cromwell who then marched up through Lincolnshire and relieved the Fairfaxes, forcing the Marquis of Newcastle to retreat towards York.

The Scots enter the war

Although the crisis in England had started with the quarrel between the King and the Covenanters, the Scots had, until now, remained neutral. But months of careful diplomacy by Pym paid off. The Scots were alarmed at the King's successes and at the rumours that an army of hated Irish Catholics would be brought over. They feared that if the King won in England he would turn his attention to Scotland next.

In return for payment and a promise that a Scottish-style Calvinist Church would be established in England after the war, the Scots agreed to invade on Parliament's side. A committee of Parliament's leaders and Covenanters, called the Committee of Both Kingdoms, was set up to run the war. But it was Pym's last act. On 8 December 1643 he died and was buried in Westminister Abbey. To him more than anyone else Parliament owed its survival and ultimate victory, and in the difficult years following his death many were to regret the loss of his guiding vision and organizational genius.

Marston Moor

By the spring of 1644 it was the Royalists who found themselves hard pressed. The King had ordered his Lord Deputy in Ireland to make peace with the Irish rebels as quickly as possible and recruit an army to send over to England. In expectation of this Rupert was in the north-west, securing ports for the invasion, but he was worried by the situation elsewhere. The Scots had joined up with Fairfax and Manchester in May and the three combined armies, numbering some 25,000 men, now laid siege to York where the Marquis of Newcastle was trapped. In the south it looked as if the armies of Essex and Waller were closing in on the King at Oxford. In alarm Charles wrote to his nephew ordering him to go immediately to the relief of York and then come to his own rescue.

As Rupert marched with all speed for York the besiegers withdrew to cut him off. But he out-manoeuvered them, reaching the city from the north. By his quick thinking the city had been saved without a shot being fired and Newcastle wrote to him calling him 'the redeemer of the north and saviour of the crown'.

In reply Rupert sent the Marquis a curt order to meet him at four o'clock the next morning to cross the river and attack the enemy. With his troops worn out after a long siege and he himself insulted by this off-hand treatment by someone half his age, Newcastle failed to appear. By the time he joined the Prince it was four in the afternoon and Parliament's forces had had time to draw up and prepare for battle. The Prince had missed his chance.

The armies stood facing each other on Marston Moor until half past seven that evening. Then, with only half an hour of daylight left, Rupert mistakenly concluded there could be no battle and started to dismiss his cavalry. Oliver Cromwell, commanding Parliament's horse opposite, chose this moment to attack and the pride of Rupert's Cavaliers were routed. On the opposite flank George Goring fared better and in turn broke Fairfax's cavalry, but once again the Cavaliers went charging off the field leaving their infantry unprotected. It was here that Cromwell's discipline and training showed. Keeping his troopers

Map showing the sites of major battles.

together he now charged the Royalist infantry on the flank. By the time Goring's cavalry started to return it was too late. Only Newcastle's Whitecoats, the stout Yorkshiremen, remained on the field, fighting to the death far into the night.

Newcastle himself went into exile in shame. Rupert rallied what soldiers he could to fight another day, but the north was lost. More significantly the Royalist cavalry had for the first time been defeated and a new star was rising on the Parliamentary side. Cromwell's Ironsides, given the name it is said by the defeated Prince himself, were beginning to pull their weight.

7 FROM MARSTON MOOR TO NASEBY

Rupert's haste, which cost him so dear at Marston Moor, arose from the belief that his uncle was about to be surrounded by Waller and Essex at Oxford. In fact he need not have worried. By the time the great battle was fought, Essex had disobeyed his orders and marched off to the south-west, where he succeeded in getting cut off and lost his entire army. He himself escaped to blame Waller loudly for not supporting him. As winter approached and Parliament's armies gathered in the Thames Valley, a more serious quarrel between Manchester and Cromwell broke out.

Oliver Cromwell, the Member of Parliament and army leader who came to rule England as Lord Protector from 1653 until his death in 1658.

The uniforms of various ranks of soldiers in Cromwell's army. The New Model Army soon became the main political power in the country.

The Self Denying Ordinance

Manchester seemed to lose all enthusiasm for the war, as if he feared victory as much as defeat. In reality it was Cromwell's Ironsides he feared. Against all the social conventions of the time, Cromwell had been promoting men of low birth as officers. They were men, he claimed, of spirit, who were totally committed to the war against the King: 'I had rather have a plain russet coated captain that knows what he fights for and loves what he knows,' said Cromwell, 'than what you call a gentleman and is nothing else.'

Men like Manchester began to realize that their war against the King was also damaging the social order upon which their own positions as peers of the realm depended. If the King were destroyed, might not the peers be next to go? But if the King regained his power their situation would be equally desperate. Manchester complained in despair: 'If we fight [the King] a hundred times and beat him ninety-nine times, he will be King still. But if he beat us but once, or the last time, we shall be hanged, we shall lose our estates and our posterities

Sir Thomas Fairfax, who commanded the New Model Army, withdrew into private life five years after the execution of Charles I.

be undone.' As Cromwell pointed out, it was really an argument for not starting the war in the first place.

That winter, when the two generals took their quarrel to Westminster, Cromwell came out on top. A measure was passed through Parliament preventing any member from holding an army command. On the surface this Self Denying Ordinance seemed a fair way to divide Parliament's military and political power, but underneath it was more subtle. As life peers Essex and Manchester were permanently barred from the army, whereas Cromwell could always resign his seat in the Commons and remain a general. In fact this was not necessary. He had enough support in the House to persuade them to make an exception to their new rule and was petitioned to go on fighting.

The New Model Army

Over the winter both sides tried to reform their armies. Until now most troops had been recruited locally and it was difficult to persuade them to fight outside their own areas. Hopton's Cornishmen had gone home after the fall of Bristol and refused to fight elsewhere in the country. But already Parliament's finances were stronger than the King's. Like the King, the Parliamentary leaders collected forced loans and confiscated the estates of their enemies. But they also levied a very lucrative Excise Tax on all goods sold in the areas they controlled. Their administration was also more efficient, but here again the pressures of war were bringing about alarming social changes. Committees had been set up in each county to collect money and raise troops and many who sat on them were of lower social origins than the traditional county rulers, who were often unwilling to plunder their neighbours and fellow gentlemen.

By 1644 the money raised by the county committees was being pooled centrally in London, rather than being spent locally, and this allowed Parliament to set up a truly national army. The New Model Army was an amalgamation of the local forces, but its 22,000 men were paid promptly and at standard rates. With Fairfax in command and Cromwell as Lieutenant-General of Horse, the New Model Army soon acquired an identity of its own with its soldiers putting allegiance to the army above local loyalties. These were the men who were not only to win the war, but also to become the main political force in the country afterwards.

Prince Rupert, now commander-in-chief of the King's forces, was also trying to unify his command. Unfortunately he was given no support by the King, who continued to allow almost complete independence to the other commanders in the south and west. No central administration was set up and, bolstered by his ever optimistic new favourite, George Digby, Earl of Bristol, the King continued to put his hopes in the imminent arrival of an Irish Catholic army. In fact negotiations with the rebel Irish had broken down. The only effect of the King's plans was to alienate many potential friends and harden the resolve of his enemies, who now started hanging any Irishmen who fell into their hands. The war was becoming more vicious.

At the Battle of Naseby, in 1645, the Ironsides under Cromwell and Fairfax inflicted a heavy defeat on the Royalists.

Naseby

The great testing of the New Model Army came in June 1645. Cromwell and Fairfax had split up and Rupert now marched north with the main Royalist army, hoping to draw Fairfax after him and to isolate him. He ordered Goring in the south-west and Gerrard in Wales to meet him in the Midlands. In fact the opposite happened. Goring ignored the Prince's orders and stayed in Bath, and Gerrard failed to arrive from Wales. On the other hand Cromwell and Fairfax successfully met up and, with an army twice the size of the King's, marched to give battle.

Rupert was against fighting on such unfavourable terms, but he was overruled by the King's other advisers, led by Digby. This would be the battle to end all battles he claimed. So on the morning of 15 June the two armies found themselves facing each other near the little village of Naseby.

This time Rupert started the battle with a devastating charge. But although the regiments which took the force of the attack on both wings broke and fled, far more had been held in reserve. Soon weight of numbers began to tell and the Cavaliers, battered by repeated charges from Cromwell's Ironsides, broke and fled. By one o'clock in the afternoon there was 'not a horse or man of the King's army to be seen except the prisoners'.

Rupert recognized the defeat for the disaster it was and now urged the King to make strong his remaining territory in the south-west and to negotiate from there. But Charles could not believe that God would desert him. In a letter to Rupert he admitted his cause might look desperate to a soldier or statesman, 'Yet as a Christian I must tell you, that God will not suffer rebels and traitors to prosper, nor this cause to be overthrown.'

Meanwhile the New Model Army had marched quickly down to the south-west. In July Goring was routed at Langport and by mid August Rupert was preparing a last desperate defence of Bristol. Charles hoped winter would bring relief from attack and, of course, help from Ireland. He also looked north to Scotland where his new champion, the Marquis of Montrose, was winning a miraculous string of victories.

Montrose

Montrose's campaign in Scotland started after Marston Moor, with the news that 1,100 Irish had landed in the Scottish Highlands. Unable to march through the hostile lowlands in any force, Montrose reached the Irish in disguise and persuaded their leader to declare for the King. He then started on a campaign which was to make him master of Scotland in less than a year. Montrose showed himself to be a genius of guerrilla warfare. He would emerge from the mountains, take a

Covenanter armies chased Montrose through the Highlands. In the 1650s he was caught and executed for his leadership in the Royalist cause.

city like Perth or Aberdeen and then once again disappear into the mists. All through the winter of 1644 he was chased by Covenanter armies through the Highlands. He ravaged the Campbell lands, whose chief the Earl of Argyll was also the leading Covenanter. In freezing weather he marched through some of the roughest country in Scotland, and when Argyll thought him dead from cold, appeared over the shoulder of Ben Nevis, the highest mountain in the country, and routed the Covenanter army below. By August 1645 Montrose had inflicted six devastating defeats on larger Covenanter armies and now, with all Scotland before him, he planned to march to the King's aid in England. Well could King Charles believe in miracles.

8 THE END OF THE CAVALIERS

By 1645 the years of disrupted harvests and markets, pillaging, forced loans and quarter (billeting) were causing serious unrest among the common people. Although they had had nothing to do with the original dispute, it was they who paid the price of the war. This unrest now showed itself in an alarming form.

The Clubmen

In at least ten different counties the common people armed themselves with what they could and formed into associations to defend themselves against both sides. The majority of the Clubmen, as they were called, were probably peasants and small land-holders or yeomen, although in a few areas the leaders seem to have been minor gentry. The movement was strongest in disputed areas where the armies had passed most frequently, especially the south-west. In Dorset and Wiltshire they claimed to be able to raise 20,000 men at forty-eight hours' notice, although no force this size ever materialized.

The demands drawn up by this third force show they had neither interest in, nor understanding of, the war. They wanted the armies to leave their areas, and a return to the rule of the law and traditional ways of local government. Neither side understood the Clubmen and both tried to enlist their help. Goring had some initial success in Devon, providing them with arms. But he could not control the excesses of his soldiers and the Clubmen turned hostile. After Langport many of the fleeing Royalists were slaughtered by the peasants they had themselves armed.

Helped by the good discipline of the New Model Army, Fairfax had more success in allaying the fears of the Clubmen. But where he could not conciliate he fought. In Dorset and South Wales large gatherings of Clubmen were routed at the first charge of the Ironsides. The movement itself disintegrated at the end of the war when the main grievances disappeared.

The end of the Cavaliers

In September 1645 the King's cause suffered two irreversible defeats within the space of three days. Although he had promised he could

Prince Rupert at the siege of Bristol: he hoped to hold the city for months but surrendered it to Parliament after only three weeks.

hold out for several months, Rupert surrendered Bristol after a siege of only three weeks. Many of the forts in the outer defences had been cut off, and more seriously, the well in the citadel was cracked. With no water, resistance could only be short. Rupert was allowed to march out with all his men, but they left their firearms, including nearly 100 cannon.

Charles never forgave his nephew for the surrender of Bristol. Believing the whisperings of Digby, he thought Rupert had deliberately betrayed him. Rupert later went into exile, but even after the King's death he continued to harry the Parliamentary navy with a small squadron of ships in the name of Charles II.

Three days after the fall of Bristol, Montrose was defeated. He had been unable to persuade many of his Highlanders to march south to England. Before he reached the border his movements were betrayed and he was surprised by a much larger Parliamentary force. Montrose himself was persuaded to escape with his small group of cavalry, but his Irish infantry were surrounded and eventually surrendered in return for their lives. But the Calvinist ministers were not satisfied with this. First the camp followers, the women and boys, were massacred and then most of the men were hanged or drowned.

One by one the last Royalist strongholds now surrendered. The south-west fell and the King's eldest son Charles, Prince of Wales, fled to the Channel Islands. His father continued to hold court at Oxford through the winter, but there was no hope of relief.

In March Lord Astley, who had commanded the King's infantry at Edgehill, surrendered the last Royalist field army. 'You have done your work boys,' said the old Cavalier to his captors, 'you may go play, unless you fall out among yourselves.' His words proved to be prophetic. Towards the end of April 1646 Charles left Oxford in disguise. A week later he surrendered to the Scots Covenanter army which had been fighting in England, hoping to exploit the divisions which were now emerging amongst his enemies.

Presbyterians and Independents

When the Puritans had been persecuted by Laud in the 1630s their common opposition to the King had obscured their differences. Now, with Charles defeated, alarming divisions began to emerge.

King Charles escaping from the city of Oxford in disguise in 1646.

A week after fleeing Oxford, Charles (on horseback) surrenders to the Scots Covenanter army.

At the centre of Protestant thought was the doctrine of the 'Priesthood of all Believers', which held that any man could reach God directly through studying the Bible, without the need of priests, saints and ceremonies to act as intermediaries. When Luther first expounded this idea, over 100 years before, it had opened a Pandora's box of radical ideas and many different sects broke away from the original movement, setting up their own Churches. Calvin's Church at Geneva had come

The Levellers found support amongst the ordinary people of London and the New Model Army but were satirized (as here) by their opponents.

almost as a reaction to this burst of free-thinking, once again restoring order with a rigid structure of ministers and elders to enforce uniformity, uphold public morals and interpret the 'true' religion. The Presbyterian Church structure, as Calvin's system was called, had been copied closely in Scotland, and by the agreement of 1643 which brought the Scots into the war, Parliament had agreed to set up a similar Church in England.

But the idea of a strict new Church and doctrine being enforced was as abhorrent to many Englishmen as the Laudian Church had been, and for exactly the same reason. Taking the doctrine of Priesthood of all Believers to its logical conclusion, they wanted the freedom to practise their own ideas and choose their own preachers and ministers. The champion of the Independents, as they were called, was none other than Oliver Cromwell. Along with his son-in-law Henry Ireton and others in the army, he called for religious freedom for those with 'tender consciences' and warned that his men had not fought so hard to be enslaved by a rigid Presbyterian Church.

To the Presbyterians, both in Scotland and in England, the idea of religious toleration was equally abhorrent. Men like Denzil Holles, the leader of the Presbyterians in the Commons, and the Earl of Manchester in the Lords, were very conservative in their outlook and believed an ordered Church was necessary to maintain order in society. They were deeply alarmed at the bewildering array of religious and political ideas which circulated in the climate of freedom produced by the war.

The Levellers

The Presbyterians had good cause to be alarmed. As a result of the war it was as if all the restraints which had held society together were suddenly lifted. Whilst Independent preachers thundered against the Presbyterians from the pulpits of London, thousands of pamphlets were sold on the streets. Some declared the second coming of Christ was imminent and that the rule of the saints would be established in England. Others started to attack the privileges of the wealthy and called for political reforms which would give power to the common people.

The strongest calls for political change came from John Lilburne, nicknamed 'Freeborne John'. In pamphlets such as *England's Birthright* he voiced the resentments of many common Londoners against the wealthy merchants, lawyers and aldermen who were still their masters. Along with his friend William Walwyn, he was to organize a political party called the Levellers which called for genuinely revolutionary changes in the social order and in government. The Levellers not only found many recruits amongst Londoners, but more importantly amongst the rank and file of the New Model Army.

The Scots and the King

For most of 1646 the Scots did their best to convert the King to Presbyterianism, but Charles steadfastly refused to take the Covenant, believing the Scots would eventually support him against the hated Independents anyway. In this belief he was wrong and at the end of the year the Scots gave up, handing the King over to Parliament in return for the payment of their troops. They had, it was reported, sold their King. At the end of 1646 the Presbyterian party in England still had a fragile majority in the Commons and the Scots hoped they would reach a settlement with the King before more radical ideas overtook them.

9 THE WORLD TURNED UPSIDE DOWN

Although the initial aim of the war—to bring the King home to his 'Loving Parliament'—had been achieved, no settlement had been reached as to the future government of the country. Whilst the Presbyterian majority in the Commons tried desperately to bring Charles to terms, the army was growing more and more restless. By 1647 it was many months since the soldiers had been paid. They had little to do except listen to the hundreds of preachers who flocked to the camps, and discuss the ideas of the Levellers and others who wanted radical changes in government. Meanwhile the Presbyterians, who Cromwell reported had 'So much malice against the army as besots them,' debated how to get rid of this rising menace.

Parliament and the army

In February 1647 Parliament voted that the army should be disbanded without arrears of pay, with only those who would serve in Ireland being re-enlisted. The decision provoked an immediate revolt by the rank and file with both the cavalry and infantry regiments electing delegates, or 'Agitators', to represent them. By May, when the Commons belatedly voted six weeks' arrears of pay and sent Cromwell and three other MPs along to negotiate, the soldiers were in open mutiny and most of their officers were supporting them. Far from negotiating, Cromwell now joined the army, claiming he did so to maintain its unity and prevent the situation getting out of control. In desperation the Presbyterians in Parliament once again ordered the army to disband and made plans to send the King to Scotland, from where they hoped he would return with the Covenanters to defeat their own New Model Army. But they were too late.

At the end of May, Cornet Joyce (a cornet was the lowest rank of officer in the army) went with 500 men to seize the King and take him to Hampton Court, under army control. Refusing to disband, the army gathered at Newmarket. A 'General Council' made up of generals, officers and ordinary soldiers was set up. It accused the leading Presbyterian MPs of treason and agreed to march on London.

As Lord Protector, Cromwell was almost as powerful as the King had been – a fact which dismayed radicals.

It is doubtful whether Cromwell, or any of the other generals, were still in control. The Agitators had been heavily influenced by the Levellers and wanted to dissolve Parliament and set up a new constitution. In vain Cromwell urged restraint. The Presbyterian MPs accused of treason now fled, and in August the army occupied the capital.

The Putney Debates

It was now Cromwell's turn to try and find a settlement with the obstinate King. Although he advocated religious freedom, as a large landowner Cromwell was politically conservative, believing some form of monarchy was essential for stability of property and the social order.

This conservatism was evident in a new constitution, called 'The Heads of Proposals' drafted by Ireton and Cromwell in July. It proposed a small change only in the franchise (i.e. those with the right to vote in the elections to the Commons). It also proposed a modified Church with bishops, but allowed religious freedom for those who did not want to join, and it demanded an end to the abuses of the 1630s. New Parliaments were to be elected every two years. The House of Lords and the office of king were to be retained.

Meanwhile the Agitators in the army put forward their own constitution based on the ideas of the Levellers. 'The Agreement of the People' called for all men to be able to vote in the elections to the House of Commons, Parliaments to be summoned every three years and the abolition of the House of Lords. The King was nowhere mentioned. It was a remarkable document but only in this century have any of its revolutionary proposals been realized.

A contemporary drawing of Charles as a prisoner on the Isle of Wight.

Colonel Pride made way for the execution of the King by ridding the House of Commons of Presbyterians.

In the autumn the two sets of proposals were debated in the army camp at Putney. Cromwell staunchly defended the propertied franchise (that only those men with property should take part in Parliamentary elections), declaring that The Agreement of the People did 'lead much to anarchy'. But he and Ireton were defeated when at the beginning of November the Army Council voted for an extension of the franchise to all except servants. On the same day they called for a general rendezvous of the army so that the united strength of the regiments could ensure the decision was put into effect.

For a brief period it looked as if there might be a genuine revolution, but the Agitators' plans were shattered by the escape of the King. Once again the spectre of civil war arose and in the general alarm the generals were able to reassert control. The escape of the King played so perfectly into Cromwell's hands that many suspected him of organizing it, especially when Charles surrendered to Cromwell's cousin on the Isle of Wight.

But the King's escape was followed by a new crisis. In December he made an agreement with the Scots who agreed to invade England on his behalf. The army now united to meet this new threat, pledging to bring Charles, that 'Man of Blood', to justice.

The Second Civil War

In the early summer of 1648 there were Royalist risings in South Wales, Essex and Kent, in expectation of the Scottish invasion. Half the fleet, which had been loyal to Parliament throughout the war, also declared for the King. Although large numbers of men took up arms, they were poorly led and disunited, and the support from Scotland was very slow in arriving. By the time the Scots, led by the Duke of Hamilton, crossed the border in July, the rebellion in Kent had fizzled out and Cromwell had defeated the rebels in South Wales. Only Colchester in Essex still held out against Fairfax.

Cromwell marched north to meet the invaders who outnumbered him by two to one. However, Hamilton was very inefficient and failed to keep his army together. As he approached the city of Preston, his forces were strung out over nearly 26 km (16 miles). In a series of

The Rump Parliament: with the Presbyterians removed, all that remained of the Commons was 'the rump and dregs' seen here in a satirical cartoon.

The trial of Charles I (seated in the foreground).

battles around Preston, Cromwell routed his divided enemies. Three days later Colchester surrendered after a bitter siege of nearly two and a half months. In his anger at the renewed bloodshed Fairfax shot the two Royalist leaders.

The King condemned

With the soldiers away fighting, the Presbyterians in Parliament once again reasserted their majority and tried to persuade the King to accept their terms. They wanted him to give up the right to command the army, to accept a Church of their choosing and allow his principal supporters to be banished. But the King refused any settlement. Instead he continued his plans to escape, writing to his son that his negotiations were only to allow him to gain time to divide his enemies. Charles's double-dealing arose not from dishonesty, but from the conviction that it was his duty before God to preserve his sovereign authority. He would rather die than forsake what he regarded as a God-given trust.

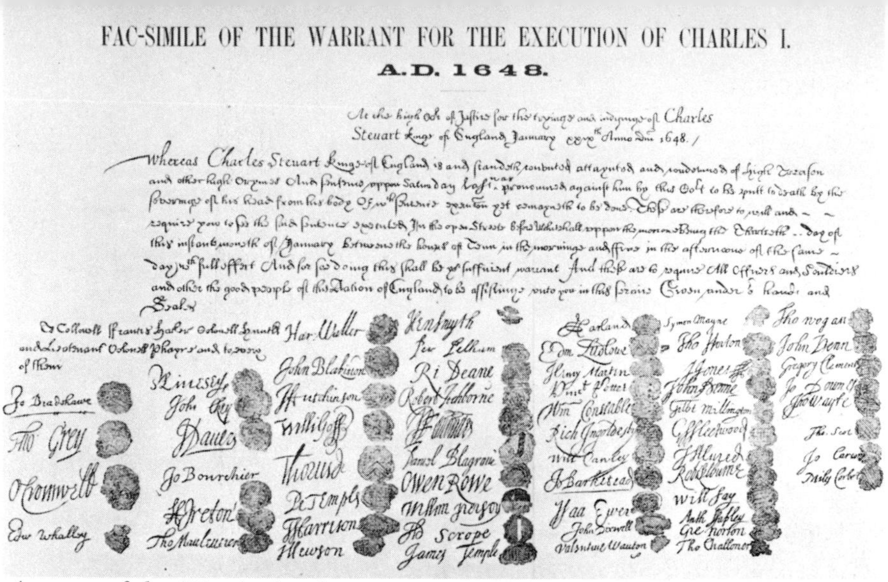

FAC-SIMILE OF THE WARRANT FOR THE EXECUTION OF CHARLES I.

A.D. 1648.

A copy of the King's death warrant, with the signatures of the 'Regicides'.

On 16 November the Army Council of Officers called for the death sentence against the King. While Cromwell was still mopping up Royalist resistance in the north, his son-in-law Ireton marched on London and occupied the capital for the second time. The generals then made sure of Parliament. Colonel Pride went to Westminster and threw out the Presbyterians, and their leaders were locked up. When Cromwell came south he expressed satisfaction at Pride's Purge of Parliament.

The remainder of the Commons, who became known as The Rump, then nominated 135 commissioners to sit in a High Court of Justice and try the King 'in the name of and on behalf of the people of England'. Under English law all justice had always been assumed to come from the King, but now the Commons turned this principle upside down, claiming that the people, not the King, were the source of all just power. Charles, they said, had abused the trust placed in him by the people by making war on his subjects.

When the trial opened, in Westminster Hall in January 1649, about half the commissioners, including Fairfax, stayed away. The King defended himself with great ability, refusing to recognize the authority of the court. He claimed that he himself stood for the 'Liberty of the People of England', and that the power now trying him was the arbitrary force of the army, not the will of the people. But the court took his refusal to accept their authority as an admission of guilt. When the commissioners retired to consider the sentence Cromwell is said to have shouted down the waverers. Fifty-nine of them, the Regicides as they were called, signed the death warrant. When the court reassembled the King heard himself declared guilty and the sentence was passed 'that the said Charles Stuart, as a Tyrant, Traitor and Murderer and a Public Enemy, shall be put to death, by the severing his head from his body.' Three days later the sentence was carried out.

10 THE COMMONWEALTH AND BEYOND

The execution of Charles I solved few of the problems which had caused the Civil War and Cromwell was now faced with the question of how to replace the role played by the King. More immediately the Levellers were still a threat, the Irish rebellion was still in full swing and the Scots were furious at the execution of their King.

Ireland and Scotland

Immediately after the death of Charles a Council of State was set up by the Commons to run the country with Cromwell as Chairman. A Commonwealth was declared and the Monarchy and the House of Lords were formally abolished. Meanwhile the preparation of an army

An Irish castle being captured in 1641: eight years later Cromwell conducted a bloody and brutal campaign against the Catholic Irish.

Cromwell storming the Irish town of Drogheda: he distributed Irish land among Protestant settlers at this time.

to go to Ireland was used as an opportunity to crush the Levellers. John Lilburne and the other leaders were arrested and when the soldiers in London mutinied, their ringleader, Robert Lockyer, who had fought throughout the war, was shot. Despite this there was another more serious mutiny in May, which was only supressed after a lightning night attack by Cromwell, who had four more ringleaders shot. The main cause of the mutinies was a refusal to fight in Ireland because, unlike most of the English upper classes, the Levellers regarded the Irish as fellow sufferers against oppression.

Cromwell's attitude was very different, and his Irish campaign of 1649–50 was conducted with extreme brutality. In order to instil the fear of God into the native population the first two towns which were captured, Drogheda and Wexford, were sacked and several thousand soldiers, priests and civilians were butchered. Cromwell's religious toleration did not extend to Irish Catholics. With the rebellion crushed, large amounts of land were confiscated and given to English Protestant settlers who had lent money to Parliament over the preceding years. In this way it was the Irish who paid for Parliament's victory. The memory of Cromwell's campaign and the colonization which followed have caused bitterness and division in Ireland ever since.

After Ireland Cromwell turned his attention to Scotland, where Charles's eldest son had been proclaimed Charles II. In the late summer of 1650 Cromwell marched north and routed one Scots army at Dunbar.

Exactly a year later he caught up with Charles, who had invaded England. At the battle of Worcester the Royalist army was smashed and Charles only escaped the country by disguising himself. Once again Cromwell emerged victorious from the third civil war to shake the country in less than a decade.

But the conquests did not stop there and Cromwell now turned to broader designs. An aggressive commercial war against the Dutch was followed by a longer war against the traditional Spanish enemy. Inheriting the interests of the pre-war Providence Island Company, Spanish possessions in the Caribbean were attacked and a permanent colony was established in Jamaica. Suddenly, after years of weakness, England was regarded as a major European power. More than anyone else it was Cromwell who laid the foundations of Britain's later imperial strength.

After Cromwell had dealt with Ireland he turned his attention to the Scots, whom he defeated at the Battle of Dunbar in 1650.

A Dutch satirist's view of Oliver Cromwell (fourth from left) dissolving Parliament.

The Lord Protector

For Cromwell, 1653 was the high point of the revolution. Like most men in the seventeenth century he believed all history was part of a Divine plan. He saw the hand of God in his victories and believed he had been chosen as an instrument to act out God's will on earth. The more he succeeded the more he believed he was preparing for some Divine revelation, perhaps the setting up of a perfect Godly society in England. In this he was heavily influenced by religious radicals in the army, such as Colonel Harrison, who believed the second coming of Christ was imminent. To institute this Utopia Cromwell expelled the Rump Parliament and put in its place a Godly assembly of 140 men, to whom he resigned all his power.

But, alas, the Barebones Parliament (as this assembly became known) proved to be as divided as all its predecessors. Whilst the radicals set about drawing up far-reaching reforms, the conservatives grew alarmed at what they feared would be an attack on property. At the end of the year they gained the upper hand and, dissolving themselves, they handed back power to Cromwell, who was declared Lord Protector and given many of the powers the King had once enjoyed.

But Cromwell was now a disillusioned man, no longer interested in revolution. The Protectorate marked a full return to conservative values with the protection of property at the top of the list. The radicals, both religious and political, refused to accept the new régime. Several

Parliaments were called, although they were not very co-operative, and eventually Cromwell took to ruling directly through the army, with major-generals being given specific areas of the country to control. When Cromwell died in 1658 the régime had lost most of its popularity and few were prepared to support his son Richard.

The Restoration

The traditional landed rulers of the country were by now sick of the army and the financial burdens it placed on them, wanting rather a return to traditional forms of local government. In May 1660 one of Cromwell's commanders, General Monk, took over and recalled the Rump of the Long Parliament. They declared Charles II King and at the end of the month he returned to take up his crown, to the peal of church bells and scenes of rejoicing.

Along with the Monarchy, the House of Lords and the Church were also restored and the old Royalists who had fought in the war were rewarded. However, there was no general revenge; an 'Act of Indemnity and Oblivion' was passed which gave a general pardon to all except the Regicides, who had signed Charles I's death warrant. Nine of these

Cromwell's investiture as Lord Protector: this dismayed the radicals who had hoped for a revolutionary new political system.

who were caught now suffered the horrible fate of being hanged, drawn and quartered.

But the Restoration did not solve the problems with Parliament. Taxation and religion continued to cause conflict and there was nearly another civil war in 1680 when the opposition in Parliament tried to get Charles's Catholic brother James excluded from the succession to the throne. They were defeated, but only after very clever manoeuvering on the part of Charles II.

The development of the Constitution

The experience of Charles I had shown the power of the English Political Nation to get rid of a king they did not like. When James II tried to spread Catholicism, against the staunch prejudices of most of his subjects, that power was again exerted. In the 'Glorious Revolution' of 1688 James was deposed and his daughter Mary, along with her Protestant husband William of Orange, put in his place. The settlement

Richard Cromwell, Oliver's son, became Protector after his father but was unequal to the task and soon returned to obscurity.

King Charles II, recalled from exile in France, enters London in triumph as the monarchy is restored at the request of Parliament.

which followed was remarkably similar to the one suggested by Cromwell and Ireton in 1647. It provided for annual sessions of Parliament with elections every three years, an Anglican Church with bishops, but toleration for those who did not want to join it, and an agreement that taxation could be levied only with Parliamentary consent. An additional rule barred any Catholic from becoming king.

The final principle at stake in the civil war—who should appoint the king's ministers—was only gradually settled over the following centuries. Britain still has no written constitution, and present constitutional practice has evolved only slowly, with the monarchy gradually relinquishing its various powers to ministers who have the support of Parliament. But the crucial event which started that evolution and prevented an absolute monarchy being set up, where the king would have total power as he did in France, was the defeat and execution of Charles I by his Parliament.

GLOSSARY

Absolute monarchy Form of monarchy where the king (or queen) has total power.
Anglican A member of the Church of England.
Attainder A Bill of Attainder called for someone's execution for treason.
Bill A piece of legislation proposed by Parliament. If passed, it becomes an Act of Parliament and thus part of the law of the land.
Covenant The Calvinist document laying down the principles of the Church of Scotland.
Divine Right of Kings Theory that the authority of a monarch comes directly from God.
Franchise The right to vote.
Free quarter System whereby civilians were forced to give soldiers free food and accommodation.
Hierarchy An organization with ranks and classes graded one above the other.
Impeachment A process whereby the Commons could accuse and prosecute someone, usually for treason.
Kirk The Church of Scotland.
Monopoly The sole right to sell or manufacture certain goods.
Ordinance A decree.
Predestination Calvinist belief that it is predestined at the beginning of time whether an individual will go to heaven or hell i.e. that people do not have free will.
Prerogative Powers permanently vested in the crown e.g. the right to declare war.
Presbyterian Member of a Calvinist church organized around Elders (ministers) who are all of the same rank, rather than a hierarchy.
Proclamation A royal order to subjects.
Regicide Someone who kills a king.
Remonstrance A strong protest.
Standard A flag.
Subsidy Tax voted by Parliament.
Traitor Someone guilty of treason.
Treason Violation of loyalty to the king or state owed by a subject, perhaps by plotting war or rebellion. High Treason is plotting to kill the king.
Utopia An imaginary state with a perfect political or social system.

DATE CHART

1625 Charles I comes to the throne.
1629 Start of the personal rule.
1637 Prayer book introduced to Scotland.
1639 First Bishops' War.
1640 Short Parliament. Second Bishops' War. Start of the Long Parliament.
1641 Trial and Execution of Strafford. Irish rebellion. Grand Remonstrance.
1642 Attempt to arrest the five Members of Parliament. King raises his standard at Nottingham. Battle of Edgehill, both sides claiming victory.
1643 Royalists capture Bristol. Siege of Gloucester. Scots enter the war.
1644 Cromwell defeats Prince Rupert at the Battle of Marston Moor.
1645 Self Denying Ordinance. Creation of New Model Army. King's army defeated at Battle of Naseby.
1646 King surrenders to Covenanters. Scots hand King over to Parliament.
1647 Army seize the King and occupy London. Putney debates. Escape of King to the Isle of Wight.
1648 Second Civil War. Scots defeated by Cromwell at Battle of Preston. Pride's Purge of Parliament.
1649 Trial and execution of Charles I. Start of Cromwell's Irish Campaign.
1650 Third Civil War. Scots defeated at Battle of Dunbar.
1651 Charles II crowned King of Scotland, and defeated by Cromwell at Battle of Worcester.
1653 Failure of the Barebones Parliament. Cromwell becomes Lord Protector.
1658 Oliver Cromwell dies and is succeeded by his son Richard.
1660 Restoration of Charles II.
1688 The Glorious Revolution replaces James II with William III and Mary.

FURTHER READING

Ashley, Maurice Spotlight on *The English Civil War* (Thames & Hudson, 1974)
Cowie, Leonard W. *Trial and Execution of Charles I* (Wayland, 1972)
Gibb, C. J. *The Reformation* (Wayland, 1986)
Hill, Christopher *God's Englishman* (Penguin, 1972)
Kenyon, J. P. *The Stuarts* (Fontana, 1976)
Ollard, Richard *This War Without An Enemy* (Hodder, 1976)
Wedgewood, C. V. *The King's Peace* (Collins, 1955)
Wedgewood, C. V. *The King's War* (Collins, 1958)
White-Thomson, Stephen *Oliver Cromwell and the Civil War* (Wayland, 1984)

PICTURE ACKNOWLEDGEMENTS

The illustrations were supplied by BBC Hulton Picture Library 25, 39, 40, 57, 63, 67, 68; The Mansell Collection 10, 15, 42, 43, 44, 63, 66, 72; Mary Evans Picture Library *cover*, 11, 12, 27, 28, 34, 35, 36, 38, 41, 44, 51, 53, 55, 58, 65, 69, 73; The National Portrait Gallery 15, 16, 20, 61; Ann Ronan Picture Library 31. The map on page 46 is by Malcolm S. Walker. All other pictures are from the Wayland Picture Library.

INDEX